D0095099

FAKE SWEARS

FILTHY EXPLETIVES THAT ARE 102% CLEAN

Created and published by Knock Knock
1635-B Electric Avenue
Venice, CA 90291
knockknockstuff.com

Illustrations by Bjoern Altmann

Where specific company, product, and brand names are cited, copyright and trademarks associated with these names are property of their respective owners.

ISBN: 978-160106644-2

UPC: 825703500363

10 9 8 7 6 5 4 3

INTRODUCTION

You're sitting at a lovely brunch with your uptight in-laws, and spill a glass of Merlot down the front of your shirt.

You're carrying your nephew to his crib when you step (painfully) on one of his plastic building blocks.

The executive everyone detests is suddenly dismissed—and you are tapped to fill his position.

Exclamations rush to the tip of your tongue. And then you bite it.

Whether you are thrilled or upset, swearing is as natural as sneezing, and stifling the urge can deliver an unpleasant sense of anticlimax. But it's actually more serious than that: just as suppressing a sneeze can cause vertigo, hearing loss, or stroke, quashing a curse may be bad for your health.

Researchers suspect that humans have been cursing since we first began to speak. Indeed, our earliest recorded scrawls, over 5,000 years old, contain off-color remarks. What's more, recent research in the UK has shown that swearing can reduce pain, increase circulation, elevate endorphins, and provide "an overall sense of calm, control, and well-being," according to *Psychology Today*. Clearly, strong language is strong medicine—and should be indulged in as frequently as possible for proper mental hygiene.

And yet the moments when we can curse freely are far less numerous than those where propriety forbids free expression. So how do you swear when you can't swear? Simple: you fake swear.

Using the many phrases in this book, you may express your indignation, shock, and other outsized emotions with impunity, knowing that you and your extravagant expressions are beyond reproach. That's because every filthy, foul-minded phrase in here is 100 percent clean. You could use these phrases when meeting the Queen of England, the Pope, or Martha Stewart. You could eat off these epithets.

The expressions in this volume may be innocent words, but their hearts are guilty—and they feel incredibly satisfying to utter at precisely the right moment. Part of what makes faux-fanity such rich linguistic terrain is that you can indulge in a variety of ways. This book includes examples of the following:

1. Vintage slang (*Oh my stars and garters*)
2. Imitations of actual swears (*Holy shift key*)
3. Clean words that sound dirty as can be (*Bushtit*)
4. Nonsense words (*Great googly moogly*)
5. Words that are simply funny when used as swears (*Chimichanga*)

Each phrase is offered with possible scenarios for usage, as well as a helpful sample sentence to demonstrate appropriate grammar. Nevertheless, you should feel free to employ these phrases in any situation, creating entirely new usages for all the words in this book. Better yet, utilize *Fake Swears* as inspiration to build your own lexicon of ersatz expletives.

Now go forth and blaspheme. You're going to enjoy the @#!^$% out of it.

ALEHOLE / FOAMING ALEHOLE

- Any craft-beer snob or hipster to be found in a "tavern"
- Any such establishment where beer snobs congregate

I went to my old dive bar last Wednesday night, and it had been colonized by foaming ***aleholes.***

AMBER WAVES OF GRAIN

- When you spill beer all over your shirt or down the front of your pants
- When driving from Colorado to Missouri seems to take a week

Amber waves of grain! *I think we're still in Kansas, Toto—and have been for some time.*

ASHCAN

- When you realize you have to dig through the garbage because you're pretty sure you threw away your ATM card—not completely sure, just pretty sure
- When you try to pull a full garbage bag out of a trash can and it gets snagged and tears

Ashcan! *Why do I continue to buy trash bags at the 99-cent store?*

See also: *Shipping Fee*

ASPHALT

- When you ask your significant other, "Does this make my butt look big?" and he replies, "Umm . . . you are *so* pretty"
- When you want to show off your sweet b-ball moves but land in urgent care

> ***Asphalt!*** *That layup lasted two seconds, now I'm laid up for six weeks.*

ASPIRIN HAT

- A driver who doesn't use turn signals
- Someone whose earsplitting laughter is harshing your hangover

> *Don't be an* ***aspirin hat,*** *sweetie. Mommy has a headache.*

ASTRAL PAIN

- Your "spiritual" roommate who's actually a sociopath
- When you learn, too late, that your body is incapable of digesting mung beans

> *Sequoia skipped town without paying her last month's rent. What an* ***astral pain****.*

AY, KOMBUCHA

- When you're eating with chopsticks and can't quite get the food to your mouth
- To express sticker shock when purchasing organic produce

A $26 watermelon? ***Ay, kombucha!***

AY, PUPUSA

- When you forget to ask for hot sauce, and you've already pulled well away from the drive-through
- When you reach down to pet a cute little Chihuahua, who snaps at you

__Ay, pupusa__—I see Sir Taco's not in a cuddling mood.

BA-BA RUM

- When your sports team wins unexpectedly
- When you bowl a strike

I always bowl better when I drink. __Ba-ba rum!__

Alt: *Crotch Chop*

BABY BELUGA

- The lady who cuts in line at the all-you-can-eat seafood buffet
- Your friend's ugly infant whose pictures are all over Facebook and Instagram

My eyes tell me she's a __baby beluga__, but my heart says she's the next Gerber kid.

BABY FISHMOUTH

- A woman who has had unfortunate lip injections, or the resulting appearance of such a procedure
- When your child eats garbage, dirt, or something picked up off the ground

> ***Baby fishmouth,*** *I hope that was at least old food and not a dead bug.*

BACON BITS

- When something moves in your salad
- When you see lights flashing in your rearview mirror

> *I was only twenty miles over the speed limit.* ***Bacon bits!***

BALLCOCKS

- When you catch yourself in your zipper
- When your dinner party hosts' toilet overflows after you've used it

> ***Ballcocks****—that hand-tufted silk bathmat is never going to be the same.*

Alt: *Something about Mary*

BANDERSNATCH

- When the touring rock band you went to see runs off with your girlfriend and/or beer
- To steal girls and/or beer while on tour

They act so "indie," but they ***bandersnatched*** *me like Def Leppard, dude.*

BANANARAMA / BANANARAMAS

- When you've run through all your usual passwords, and the website you're trying to access locks your account
- When you realize that your new love interest is not merely fun-loving but actually crazy

> ***Bananaramas!*** *Doug and I finally hooked up last night—and he cried.*

BANG SHANG-A-LANG

- When you give yourself a surprisingly good haircut
- When you spot an immensely cute person

> ***Bang shang-a-lang!*** *I spy an angel by the guacamole dip.*

BARRY US BONDS

- A 'roid-raging jerk who hogs machines at the gym
- A preening braggart

> *Hey, I worked hard for these guns. You're just a big ol'* ***Barry US Bonds!***

Alt: *Cansec-hole*

BAZOOKA JOE

- A young man attempting a neo-greaser/1950s look
- When you step in a mountain of bubble gum on a hot day

> ***Bazooka Joe!*** *Why did I wear waffle-sole sneakers today of all days?*

BÉCHAMEL (*BAY-SHUH-MEL*)

- Alternate term for “whitey”
- A friend who thinks she is a much better cook than she is

> *She’s so nice, nobody can refuse her dinner invitations—but, sadly, she’s a* ***béchamel.***

BENEDICT CUMBERBATCH

- When you improperly flip a pancake
- When the paper tab on your teabag falls in your tea

> ***Benedict Cumberbatch****—I simply haven't the patience to be this clumsy.*

BIBLIOHHHH

- When a stack of books slips out of your arms in apparent slow motion
- When you realize that book you just put your coffee mug on wasn't *Harry Potter and the Prisoner of Azkaban* but a first-edition James Joyce

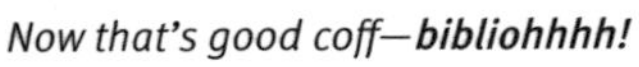

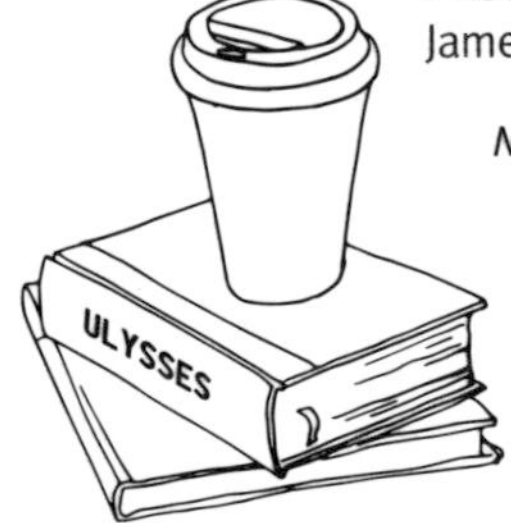

BICHON (*BEE-SHONE*)

- A person who always has the most expensive and/or trendy phone, flip-flops, or baby stroller
- To express disbelief, esp. at another's extravagance

People are paying $90,000 for those electric cars? ***Bichon!***

BLACK ANGUS

- When you attempt to carve a roast and it slips off the platter
- When a Scotsman has done you wrong

Black angus! *I was promised there would be no haggis.*

BLAH BLAH BLAHG

- A person who describes everything using Top 5 lists or only communicates through his Twitter feed
- To be uttered in response to social media–based bragging

Mindy got married in Maui to a masseur named Mike . . .
blah blah blahg.

BLANCHE, PLEASE

- When you run up against a *Golden Girls* know-it-all
- When you're battling a mime

> ***Blanche, please.*** *My "trapped in a box" has it all over your "trapped in a box."*

BLAST

- When you wake up with a hangover after the "best night ever"
- When you accidentally apply peppermint soap to your nether regions

> *This stuff smells amazing—aw,* ***blast!***

BLOW ME DOWN

- When you find out your crush is requited
- When you realize what you look like on Skype

> ***Blow me down!*** *If I were paying a per-bag fee for these eyes, they'd cost me a fortune.*

BOOBOCRAT

- Someone who is officious and exhibits a complete lack of intelligence or common sense
- Someone who leaves the cap off felt-tip pens

*Sad little Paper Mate—what **boobocrat** has done this to you?*

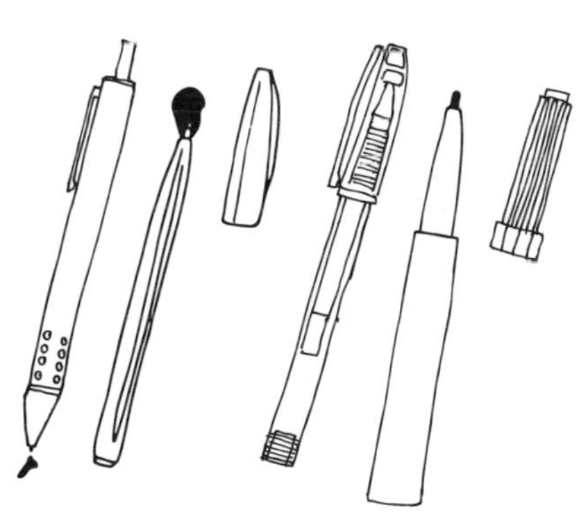

BOB CRATCHIT

- When you don't get paid for national holidays, or you must work on a holiday
- All-purpose work curse

*Temping has its advantages, but **Bob Cratchit,** who wants to work the day after Thanksgiving?*

BOLSHEVIK

- When the grocery store runs out of beets
- When, despite careful cheating, you are losing a game of *Risk*

***Bolshevik!** I had no idea Grandma was so good at this game.*

BORIS

- Your friend's boyfriend who is twenty years her senior
- A person who won't drink or smoke with you

*After graduation, Carlton became a real **Boris.***

BRADEN-HADEN-JADEN

- When you realize your child's name is on a white-trash baby name list
- When your child discovers boy bands

> ***Braden-Haden-Jaden!*** *It's going to be a long summer.*

BRAD'S ABS

- When you know you have just seriously tweaked your back doing something innocuous such as standing up or strumming an E chord
- All-purpose Pilates or core-conditioning curse

> ***Brad's abs,*** *these side bends are so boring, I just may fall asleep.*

BRONER

- When you have a crush on your brother's best friend
- A fraternity brother with hippie tendencies

> *Ian goes to Reggae on the River every year. He's a bit of a* ***broner.***

BUCKET LOVER

- When you catch your significant other cheating on you with a fruit-ice purveyor from the Renaissance Pleasure Faire
- When you order drive-through fried chicken and wind up spending $18

Bucket lover! *They even forgot the corn on the cob.*

BUCKING BRONCOS

- When you hit unexpected speed bumps or metal plates at 40+ mph
- To be uttered in appreciation of an attractive rodeo hand

Bucking broncos*, that Bo sure can wear a pair of Wranglers.*

BUSHTIT

- When someone who was going to help you move bails at the last minute
- When someone writes something inaccurate and/or unkind about you online

Bushtit! *You'd better watch your back, RandysMommy78!*

BUST MY BEATBOX

- When you're so dumbfounded by your opponent's freestyle during a rap battle that you simply must forfeit
- When your Kangol hat gets shrunk in the dryer

__Bust my beatbox,__ guess I'll have to wear my Adidas trucker cap.

CALL OF CTHULHU (*KUH-THOO-LOO*)

- When your twenty-sided die rolls under the fridge
- All-purpose ComicCon expletive

__Call of Cthulhu,__ I just met Darth Maul in the john!

CANNIBALS

- When you bite your tongue or cheek
- When you open a can of tennis balls and they spill all over the court

__Cannibals!__ I fear this does not bode well for today's match.

BY THE HORNSWOGGLE OF LORD BATTLESBY

- When you encounter excessive tangling whilst combing your muttonchops
- When you cannot find your dentures

*By the **hornswoggle of Lord Battlesby,** where's my valet when I need him?*

CASPER THE FRIENDLY GHOST

- When you are about to enter the biggest loop on the roller coaster
- When a mourner is convinced the person in the casket has moved

> ***Casper the friendly ghost!*** *Were Grandma's hands folded a minute ago?*

CHAMBER OF COMMERCE

- When your swivel desk chair suddenly breaks
- When you try, unsuccessfully, to strike up a conversation in a public restroom

> *Maybe I should have washed my hands before I tried to introduce myself.* ***Chamber of Commerce!***

CHE LE PUZO *(KAY LAY POOT-SOH)*

- All-purpose Mediterranean expression of disbelief
- When you wake up with a bloody horse's head in your bed

> ***Che le Puzo!*** *You were a good friend, old Sealy Posturepedic.*

CHEESE ON CRACKERS

- When your to-do list is wet and unreadable
- When planning a dinner for two vegans, one gluten-free pescetarian, and one raw-foodie

__Cheese on crackers__—I hope everyone tonight likes jelly beans and popcorn.

CHEESEPLATTER

- When you begin to suspect the last twenty years of your life have been a waste of time
- What you call yourself when you are too shy to mingle at a party

I could tell it was a good party, but I was a __cheeseplatter__ all night.

CHILLY WILLY

- When you get a slushie brain freeze
- Your friend who moved to Minneapolis and won't stop complaining about the snow

Hey, __Chilly Willy,__ go ice fishing on a half-frozen lake!

CHIMICHANGA

- When your margarita is served on fire
- All-purpose exclamation of appreciation or surprise at a Mexican restaurant

They didn't charge us for those extra beers. ***Chimichanga!***

CHITTY CHITTY BANG BANG

- When your car sputters, smokes, or busts a flat
- A female romantic rival who talks loud and looks cheap

*Ginny wore a bikini to Chad's party. Hello, **chitty chitty bang bang!***

CHUCKLEHEAD

- A roommate who tells Chuck Norris jokes
- A male romantic rival who talks loud and looks cheap

*Here comes that **chucklehead** Giovanni. Nice pinky ring.*

CHUNKS O' CHEESE

- All-purpose regurgitation curse
- When you are dragged to a Seal, Air Supply, or Celine Dion concert

***Chunks o' cheese**, where's good old Neil Diamond when you need him?*

CHUTES AND LADDERS

- When you hit a large pothole
- When you miss a step trying to avoid a small animal while descending stairs

> ***Chutes and ladders,*** *if this cat weren't deaf and blind, it'd be straight to the tennis-racket factory!*

COCKAPOO-SHIH

- When the groomer charges more than expected for a simple wash and cut
- When your dog insists on mounting a much larger or smaller dog at the dog park

> ***Cockapoo-shih,*** *Toto! Get off that mastiff this instant.*

See also: *Scrappy Doo*

COCKLES AND MUSSELS

- When you're held captive by Somali pirates
- When you cut your foot at the beach

> *This coral tide pool is amazing—but* ***cockles and mussels,*** *I've hit a gusher!*

CRADLE CAP

- When your infant son pees in your face
- When you run out of diapers at 10 p.m.

Cradle cap! *Do you think a dishtowel and duct tape will do till morning?*

CODPIECE

- When you realize that picturing the audience naked was a very bad idea
- When you misplace a used condom

*Aw, **codpiece**—we probably shouldn't have made out in a company car.*

CRABCAKES

- When you have an itch you can't scratch in public
- When you attend an event, expecting to be served dinner, but instead overeat tiny grilled-cheese sandwiches and mini lamb chops from hors d'oeuvres trays

*Apparently, being keynote speaker has its downside. **Crabcakes!***

CREAM OF BROCCOLI

- When you completely lose your soupspoon in your bowl
- When you discover you've had food stuck in your teeth during a meeting

***Cream of broccoli**—I hope Mr. Kincaid is far-sighted.*

CREVASSE

- When you hike to a lookout point, but hacky-sacking hippies spoil the view
- An annoying rock climber

*Yes, it's impressive that Brian has scaled El Capitan, but he's still a colossal **crevasse.***

CRIKEY

- When you hear something come out of your mouth and realize you sound exactly like your mother or father
- When you learn frightening news through a text

***Crikey.** The baby we're expecting is . . . triplets.*

CUL-DE-SAC

- When moving to the suburbs becomes inevitable
- When you take a ball to the crotch during a soccer game

***Cul-de-sac!** I've heard of taking one for the team, but I think I just took two.*

CROCKPOT

- An old grump or coot
- When you ingest something that gently roasts your brain for four to six hours

> ***Crockpot****. . . I'm not sure what was in those brownies, but that candle looks like Lionel Richie.*

CURSES

- When you have been swindled during a Victorian parlor game
- When your evil plot is foiled by a superhero

__Curses!__ My secret weather machine's been blasted to oblivion!

DACHSHUND

- A cute but unbearably annoying person
- All-purpose dog-grooming swear

__Dachshund__—I just shaved my thumb with these clippers.

DENEUVE *(DUH-NUV)*

- When you are struck with a particularly ravishing case of ennui
- French for "Be gone, peasant!"

If anyone calls, I'm taking to my bed for the foreseeable future. __Deneuve.__

DIPSTICK

- When you assume the check engine light is a suggestion
- The mechanic you found on Yelp who did $514 worth of work without giving you an estimate in advance

How did that ***dipstick*** *get four stars? He didn't even have any* Us Weeklys *in the waiting room.*

Alt: *Buttafuoco*

DORSAL FIN

- Someone who becomes seasick easily
- Someone who becomes unreasonably afraid of a shark attack while swimming in a lake or pool

Maybe a cruise wasn't such a great honeymoon idea. I forgot what a ***dorsal fin*** *I am.*

DR. HYMAN

- One whose mere presence gives you an unclean feeling
- A man who continually insists he knows what's best for a woman

Thanks, ***Dr. Hyman,*** *but I've been ordering for myself since I was seven.*

DOSE OF THE CLAP

- When you flunk your test at the free clinic
- When your spouse catches you looking up an old flame on Facebook

> ***Dose of the clap!*** *I actually just creeped* myself *out.*

DUCAL BAUBLES

- When you lose one of your great, great grandfather's solid-gold cufflinks
- When your favorite *Downton Abbey* character is killed off

> ***Ducal baubles****—as if Sunday nights weren't already depressing enough!*

DUMFUNGLE

- To handle things in a clumsy manner
- To be worn out or used up

> *Them* ***dumfungled*** *hosses best be put to pasture!*

EVIL TWEEN

- All-purpose parent-teacher conference curse
- When your attempt at trendiness misses the mark by thirteen years

__Evil tween__—I thought this ironic pop-cultural t-shirt would be a big hit at the party.

DUSTY BONES

- When you sneeze in church
- When you catch your grandmother in flagrante delicto

*O **dusty bones**—that these eyes could unsee that which they have seen.*

EAT SCHMALTZ

- When an elderly gentleman suggests you get off his lawn
- When an individual questions the nutritional value of your bacon-wrapped pork belly burrito

*I may die at 48, but I will have lived! You vegans can all **eat schmaltz!***

EFFUARY *(EFF YOU-AIRY)*

- When your kids get a snow day but your spouse doesn't
- When you drunk-text an ex on Valentine's Day

*Tell me I didn't send Chad a picture of me crying last night—aw, **effuary!***

FALKLAND ISLANDS

- Any sensitive or unresolved dispute
- When you dive into water and promptly lose your swimsuit

__Falkland Islands__—at least this water's pretty muddy.

FARTLIGHT

- All-purpose synthesizer/keyboard curse
- When you get one or more 1980s power ballads stuck in your head

__Fartlight.__ I thought "Hungry Eyes" was bad—until it morphed into "Take My Breath Away."

FATS MCGEE AND HIS DUCKIES THREE

- When you discover an overlooked Milky Way behind the wheat germ
- When you get to stay on Space Mountain for an extra ride

__Fats McGee and his duckies three__—this totally makes up for Tinkerbell not giving me her number.

FA LA LA LA LAHHH

- When your aunt insists on reciting epic poems during Christmas dinner
- When you pull the roast beef out of the oven and drop it on the floor

Our standing rib roast is now a casually leaning rib roast. ***Fa la la la lahhh.***

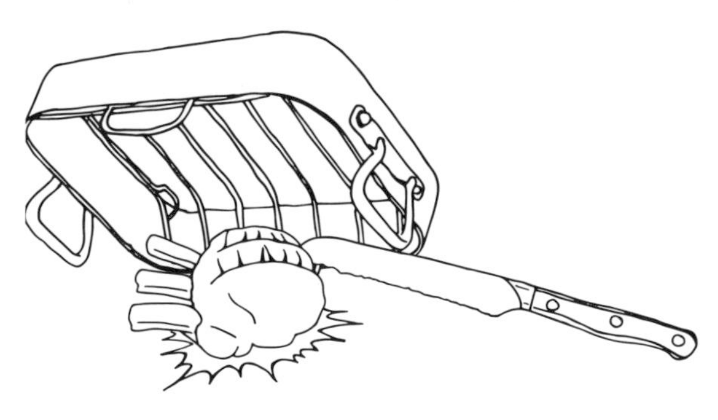

FERMEZ LA POOCH *(FAIR-MAY LA POOCH)*

- When your dog cleans himself or eats his own excrement, then licks your face
- When someone encourages her dog to pee in your yard

__Fermez la pooch,__ kind neighbor! That's not good karma—or dogma.

FICK

- When you are surprised by something disgusting coming at you, such as a booger
- When expensive organic produce is discovered to have gone rotten in less than a day

Those black mission figs I got at Whole Foods yesterday are already __ficked!__

FINGERPICKER

- When you walk through a jumbo-sized spider web and spend the next ten minutes pulling it off you
- When you inadvertently send a typo-filled text

__Fingerpicker__—I hope our landlady knows I meant "hello," not "ho."

FLAMIN' FLAXSEED

- When a homeopathic remedy miraculously clears up your acne
- When the sugar-free muffin you order at Café Agape is also flavor-free

__Flamin' flaxseed__, that reminds me of the time I ate a playing card on a dare.

FLAPJACKS

- When your breakfast falls in your lap or is stolen by a fellow cowboy
- All-purpose greasy spoon curse

__Flapjacks__, Marge! They've eighty-sixed the eggs 'n' hash!

FLEDERMAUS

- When you are too drunk to keep it up
- When you fail to hold a note while singing

***Fledermaus**. There goes my ticket to Hollywood.*

FISH FORK

- All-purpose dinner party curse
- A pretentious foodie

I could tell Carrie's new boyfriend was judging my food when we had them for dinner. That guy's a total ***fish fork.***

Alt: *Spatchcock*

FLOCK MY FIR TREE

- When you realize you simply cannot listen to "Wonderful Christmastime" by Paul McCartney—ever, ever again
- When the cut-your-own Christmas tree you have just jammed into your car begins to rustle

__Flock my fir tree,__ I don't think we're alone, Darlene.

FLUBBER

- When you keep getting junk emails that you've unsubscribed from
- When the self-checkout register keeps repeating, "An attendant has been notified to assist you"

__Flubber!__ If I'd wanted a human being to ring up my hemorrhoid cream, whiskey, and baby food, I wouldn't have chosen this line.

FLUFFERNUTTER

- When you spend several minutes roasting a marshmallow only to discover mid-bite that it is raw in the middle
- When your pillow feels wrong no matter how you rearrange it

Maybe I just need another sleeping pill. __Fluffernutter.__

FLUNK IT

- When you randomly pick an answer bubble on a clearly impossible SAT question
- All-purpose test-taking curse

A, B, C . . . let's go with D, for doomsday. ***Flunk it!***

FLUX CAPACITOR

- All-purpose time-travel curse
- When you experience uncanny déjà vu, or suspect you are in a time warp

Flux capacitor! *Did I already give dad this Sinatra box set last Christmas?*

FOR THE LOVE OF BENJI

- When you misread the parking signs, resulting in a costly ticket
- When you're folding a load of laundry with seven socks—and no mates

For the love of Benji, *I suspect our dryer contains a portal to another dimension.*

FOR THE LOVE OF HARVEY KORMAN

- When you cannot stop laughing, particularly while performing sketch comedy
- All-purpose nursing home curse

__For the love of Harvey Korman,__ your Bill Clinton impression is killing me, Grandma!

FOR THE LOVE OF JHERI

- When you put the wrong styling product in your hair
- When someone unearths an old photo of you with a dated look

> ***For the love of Jheri,*** *I do miss that roller disco.*

FRAGGLEROCK

- When you get carded outside a bar or club—though you're clearly over 35—and can't find your ID
- When you trip over a stuffed animal or other toy left on the stairs by a child

> ***Fragglerock!*** *Forget about "child-safe"—they should make these things tired dad–safe.*

Alt: *Bunny Slippers*

FRANÇOIS PÂTÉ *(FRAN-SWAH PAH-TAY)*

- A gentleman who only talks to skinny ladies at bars or parties
- A maître d' who looks you up and down and/or hassles you

> *Listen up,* ***François Pâté,*** *I made our reservation a month ago.*

FRANKINCENSE AND MYRRH

- When you are overwhelmed by Christmas decor in a home or store, esp. before Halloween
- When holiday stress drives you to the medicine and/or liquor cabinet

Frankincense and myrrh, *let's make this a Dean Martin Christmas.*

FRECKLES

- When you forget to wear deodorant
- Any bully in need of a takedown

*Hey, **freckles,** I heard you cry at* Toy Story 3.

FUNKY BUNCH

- When someone pushes their freestyle rap on you
- When you sustain a breakdancing injury

*Aw, **funky bunch!** I think I just heard my knees pop-lock.*

FUNKY WINKERBEAN

- When you realize how dumb you look attempting salsa moves in a Zumba class.
- When you slam your finger in a door

***Funky Winkerbean**—I demand we destroy this barrier and the danger it poses to all digits!*

GADZOOKS

- When you spend hours crafting a perfect response to an email and find it weeks later in your drafts file, unsent
- When your child discovers what's in your bedside table

Gadzooks! Now I know why little Tina's hands were gooey this morning.

GEEZ LOUISE

- When you are running to catch a bus, and the driver sees you but still pulls away
- When you Google something innocent—with eye-opening results

Geez Louise, I guess "Santorum" is more than just some Republican dude.

GEFILTE FISH

- To be uttered at the holiday table when you realize this is the year Grandma has finally lost her sense of taste
- When you step on something cold and gelatinous

*Oy, **gefilte fish!** I hope that was a grape.*

Alt: *Lutefisk*

GINGERSNAPS

- When you wake up next to Ron Howard but you could have sworn you went to bed with Ewan McGregor
- When your Mary Jane buckle digs into the top of your foot

Gingersnaps! *They should call these Mary pains.*

GIMCRACK

- When you have a small but pesky seed stuck between your teeth
- When you feel something break or give while working out

__Gimcrack__—normally I can't do the splits this easily.

GOOD GUMBO

- When your mother-in-law serves okra
- When your formerly cool friend debuts his new washboard band

__Good gumbo!__ I should've known something was up when he tried to show me his kazoo collection.

GRAND TETONS

- When you stare at a map, realizing you are hopelessly lost
- When you accidently brush against the front of a buxom woman

***Grand Tetons,** I'd like to scale* that *range.*

GREAT BEAVER DAMS

- When you are confronted by something of ineffable majesty or an insurmountable obstacle, such as the ocean, ever-expanding space, or a long, steep flight of stairs
- When you attempt to urinate but nothing comes out

> ***Great beaver dams,*** *how much cranberry juice is this going to take?*

Alt: *Great Lakes*

GREAT GOOGLY MOOGLY

- When you wake up to see what last night's beer goggles caused you to bring home
- To be shouted between maniacal laughs at teenage trick-or-treaters

> *If you're too cool to wear costumes, you must not want any candy.* ***Great googly moogly!***

GREAT MONOCOTS

- When you've discovered a new or rare breed of orchid
- All-purpose horticultural curse

> ***Great monocots,*** *that garden gnome is tending a* Laelia lobata*!*

See also: *Pistil and Stamen*

GREAT GODS OF THUNDER

- When your baby's digestion is more dramatic than expected
- When you declare war on the ants in your kitchen

Great gods of thunder, *the sugar bowl shall not be surrendered!*

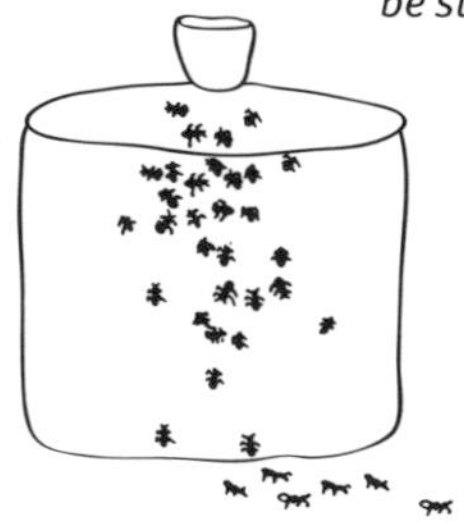

GUY LOMBARDO

- When your New Year's Eve date kisses you on the cheek at midnight
- When Great Uncle Larry kisses you on the mouth on New Year's Eve

__Guy Lombardo,__ this is no way to start a new year.

HABERDASHER / HABERDASH IT

- When the washing machine twists a load of delicates into a single Gordian knot
- When you've chosen entirely inappropriate headwear

Since when is a nun's habit not "black tie"? __Haberdash it!__

HALLIBURTON

- When you drop your ice cream cone
- When you realize the government has been sold to the highest bidder

Aw, __Halliburton__—now I suppose we'll have to mount a socialist revolution.

HAMBUNGLE

- To let burgers fall through the grill and into the fire
- To mess up a joke or anecdote

*When I **hambungled** the one about the priest, the rabbi, and the duck, I knew I'd blown the interview.*

HAM HOCKS / HONEY-GLAZED HAM HOCKS

- When you realize that your genuine leather jacket isn't
- When an unusually attractive police officer comes to break up your party

***Honey-glazed ham hocks**, I'd let that cop frisk me any night.*

HANGNAIL

- When your expensive new manicure chips
- Someone overly fond of placing blame in a work setting

*He seems nice, but you'll find that he's a real **hangnail** in a crisis.*

HASSELHOFF

- To be exclaimed during any hair-related procedure (e.g., wax job or transplant or blowout)
- All-purpose expression of frustration, esp. in bureaucratic or technological context

Hasselhoff! Now *you tell me I've been in the wrong line for the last hour?*

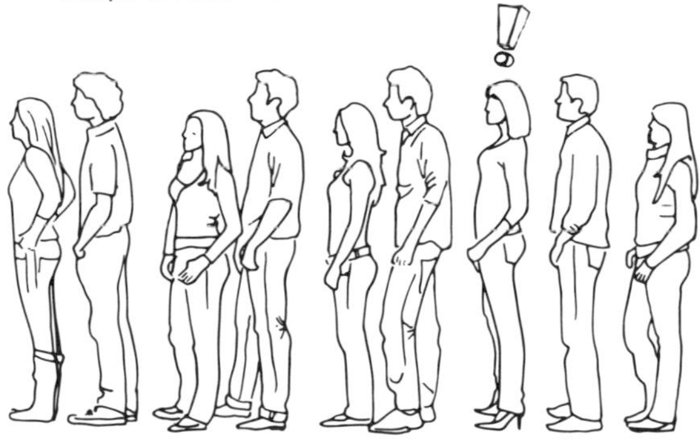

HARVEY WALLBANGER

- When you are hit so hard as to go crosseyed
- An excessively attractive person

*You said the new girl was cute, but you failed to mention that, in fact, she is a **Harvey Wallbanger.***

HEAVENS TO BETSY

- When your Bedazzler runs out of crystals
- When your aunt gives you a copy of *Fifty Shades of Grey*

***Heavens to Betsy,** I never should have told her I'm into light bondage.*

HEAVENS TO CLANCY

- When you're convinced the flower delivery van tailgating you at 80 mph is from the CIA
- All-purpose espionage expletive

***Heavens to Clancy,** I thought we had disabled that tracking device back in Monte Carlo.*

HIERONYMUS BOSCH

- When you are haunted and/or tempted by demons
- When your headache is so bad you almost start hallucinating

*These pain pills may be gold on the black market, but, **Hieronymus Bosch**, they're worthless to me!*

Alt: *Egon Schiele*

HOLY MAHOLY-NAGY

- When you meet someone who shares your passion for surrealistic photography
- When you drop a $15 sandwich on the floor at the art museum café

***Holy Maholy-Nagy**, that was the last egg salad!*

HOLY MOTHER OF MADISON

- When a minivan cuts you off in the Whole Foods parking lot
- When you're double-booked with book club and PTA—and you're late for your child's soccer practice

***Holy mother of Madison**, is it time for a second personal assistant?*

HOLY BUCKETS

- When an amateur backyard baptism goes awry
- When a lobster escapes before being cooked

***Holy buckets**, he's heading straight for the koi pond.*

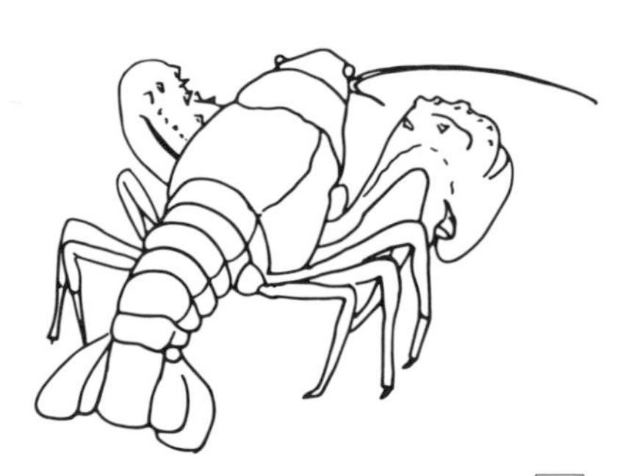

HOLY MOTHMAN PROPHECY

- When your car hits black ice on a bridge
- When your motel room is disappointing, dingy, or creepy

> ***Holy mothman prophecy,*** *that's not a "peephole," it's a bullet hole.*

HOLY RICK ASTLEY

- When your Internet date turns out to be much shorter than expected
- When your Internet date has remarkably small hands

> *His profile picture was cute, but* ***holy Rick Astley,*** *he should have been holding a cell phone for scale.*

HOLY SHIFT KEY

- When your computer freezes and/or dies
- When you mistakenly copy your supervisor on an unfortunate email

> ***Holy shift key,*** *how do I spin "Check out the boss's hideous man-purse"?*

HOT CAULKING GUN

- When your DIY bathroom rehab takes a dark turn
- When you notice an attractive male shopper at Home Depot

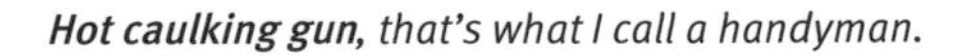

Hot caulking gun, *that's what I call a handyman.*

HOMEBORE

- Someone who wears a porkpie hat with a T-shirt
- Someone who insists he is "stayin' true to the game"

*I feel you, **homebore**, 'cause I'm just keepin' it real myself.*

HORN OF ROHAN

- When the wrong runic symbols have been engraved on your leather belt pouch
- When you detect an ill wind in a small but crowded area

***Horn of Rohan**, what I wouldn't give for a stuffy nose at this very moment.*

HOT CROSS BUTTS

- When you dance like no one's watching—but someone is
- When you have a BBQ accident

*Well doc, it's like I told the EMT, I always wanted to try grilling in the nude. **Hot cross butts**, was I wrong.*

I'LL BE A HIGGS BOSON

- What a science nerd exclaims the first time he kisses someone
- All-purpose cosmology curse or expression of surprise

__I'll be a Higgs boson,__ my calculations prove that the Big Bang exceeded the speed of light!

I'LL BE JIMMY-JAMMED

- When you're unsure what's in the burrito you just bit into
- When you get to the movies late and have to sit in the front row

__I'll be jimmy-jammed,__ I can see right up Angelina's nose.

IN YOUR HAT

- All-purpose insult or expression of dismay
- When you are being tailgated, esp. by a truck, SUV, or luxury car

The closer you get, the slower I go. That's right, buddy— __in your hat!__

JIMINY HOFFA

- When you've looked all over for something, but just can't find it anywhere
- When the donuts you bought for the office vanish during your commute

Jiminy Hoffa, *I should totally be a magician.*

JEAN BORF *(ZHONN BORF)*

- Any pretentious person
- When you're trying escargot for the first time

__Jean Borf__, thank God for garlic butter.

JIGGLIN' JELLO

- When you find your hands shaking during a date or job interview
- When you can't seem to take a non-blurry photo of your infant or pet doing something fantastic

He's playing the guitar with his feet! __Jigglin' Jello__, I hate this camera!

JIMINY CHRISTMAS

- When you turn on the light in your kitchen and see an enormous roach scuttle across the counter
- All-purpose insect curse

__Jiminy Christmas__, if the killer bees don't get us, the locusts will.

JINGLEBRAINS

- Someone who uses Christmas carols as a ringtone
- A coworker who repeatedly asks if the Internet is working for you

*Hey, **jinglebrains**, ever wonder why my name isn't Zach and I don't wear glasses? It's because I'm not the IT guy.*

JINKIES

- When you need a safety pin and can't find one
- When you receive an "emergency" phone call during a boring first date

*My roommate said the TV remote has disappeared and I have to come home right away. **Jinkies!***

JOAN CRAWFORD

- When someone steals your brilliant drag name
- When you have only wire hangers available in the closet

***Joan Crawford**, what next? Store-brand dryer sheets?*

JINX MY SPHINX

- When you give up in resignation or lose an argument
- When you experience a "lightbulb moment"

*Well, **jinx my sphinx**, I didn't know zucchini was a fruit.*

JONATHAN TAYLOR THOMAS

- When you forget the punch line mid-joke in front of a large crowd
- When the dressing comes out of the bottle way too fast, drowning your salad

__Jonathan Taylor Thomas__, get me a siphon and a bucket!

JUICEBOX

- When the truth about the Easter Bunny or Tooth Fairy is unceremoniously revealed
- A child who has a tantrum in the middle of Disney World

I wish it weren't such a small world, especially with that __juicebox__ crying in the next boat.

JUMPIN' JEHOSHAPHAT

- When you are headed over to the hummus and spy someone double-dipping
- When you or your partner has pungent garlic breath

__Jumpin' Jehoshaphat__, that baba ghanoush packs a punch.

JUNTA *(HOON-TUH)*

- Any type of genitalia, male or female
- A terrible boss, male or female

> *Her boss was such a **junta**, she considered it a mercy to be fired.*

JUPITER'S BEARD

- When you are visited by plagues or are clearly being tested by God
- When you receive divine inspiration or are giving birth

> ***Jupiter's beard**, I think I've just invented the two-in-one tuna squeezer!*

KIBBLES AND BITS

- When your pet has gone through the garbage
- When you are kicked in the groin

> ***Kibbles and bits!** If you need me, I'll be crumpled on the floor of the bathroom for the next two hours.*

KISS MY BRASS

- To be shouted upon winning an award in the presence of colleagues
- When you are laid off

I'm going to write a bestselling revenge novel that gets made into a movie with Dylan McDermott, so you losers can all ***kiss my brass!***

KLAPHAT

- Someone who routinely uses the word "irregardless"
- Someone who doesn't pull out into the intersection while making a left turn

There are ten cars behind you, ***klaphat!***

KRAKATOA EAST OF JAVA

- When you stub your toe
- When you see an amazing sight from the window of an airplane

Krakatoa east of Java! *Even from here, the Vegas Strip looks cheap and freaky.*

KISS MAYA ANGELOU

- All-purpose library curse
- When someone takes too long at the only working microfiche machine

> *Are you going to hog that 1979* Pittsburgh Post-Gazette *all day?* ***Kiss Maya Angelou!***

Alt: *Go to Heller*; *Audre Lorde*

See also: *What the Faulkner?*

KRUTTSCHNITT

- When you realize your toupee is on sideways
- When you get dangerously bad directions on a walking tour of Leipzig

> ***Kruttschnitt!*** *I fear my Saxon odyssey has taken a Wagnerian turn.*

LAND O' LAKES

- When jumping off a high dive or cliff
- When you tear your bread while spreading butter on it

> ***Land o' lakes,*** *that was the last piece.*

Alt: *Lewis and Clark*

LARGEMOUTH BASS

- When you fall into a large body of liquid, such as a pool or industrial vat of soup
- A coworker who always wants to talk about her pets, children, or health problems

> *Watch out for Belinda in accounting—since having a kid, she's become the office* ***largemouth bass.***

LEAPIN' LAPENDECTOMY

- All-purpose hospital swear
- When you realize your chiropractor is a swindler or Scientologist

Leapin' lapendectomy, I knew something was fishy when they hooked me up to that lie detector.

LITTLE FINGER

- When you are cheated by the manager of the most exclusive whorehouse in all the land
- When you are shocked by another person's manners during high tea

Little finger! That guy just dipped his scone in the clotted cream.

LOG JAMMIT

- When you are stuck in traffic
- When you are invited to join an orgy

Log jammit, I'm coming in!

LOS ZAPATOS

- When you drop your taco filling on the floor
- When you've just bitten into a habanero

Los zapatos, *I thought that was a bell pepper.*

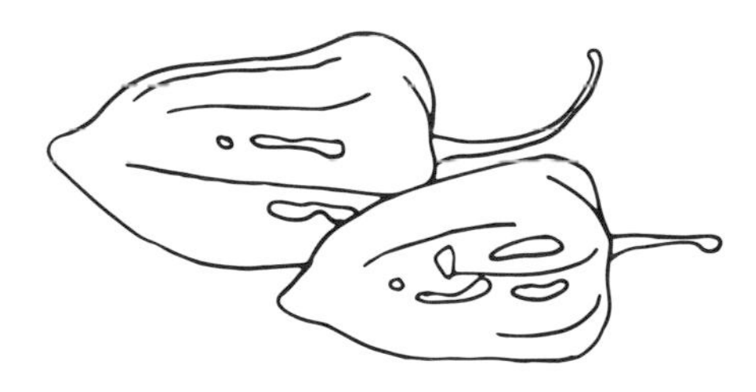

LUTEFISK

- When you find out they're serving haggis
- When you accidentally swear at your Lutheran grandmother-in-law's house

When I dropped that plate, I probably shouldn't have dropped an F-bomb. ***Lutefisk!***

MACARONI DINNER

- When your crash diet involves eating cottage cheese past 5 p.m.
- When you find a cashmere sweater at Barneys for 75 percent off

Macaroni dinner, *this must be my lucky day.*

MADAME TUSSAUD

- When you see what's on the end of your cotton swab
- All-purpose cosmetic surgery curse

Madame Tussaud, *for a second I thought Auntie Griselda was doing Jack Nicholson as the Joker.*

MAHLER FLOGGER

- When someone is opening a cough drop wrapper during a performance
- Someone who continually references high culture

*With Debbie, it's always "Goethe" this and "Velazquez" that. She's such a **Mahler flogger.***

MAMMA MIA THATSA SPICY MEATBALL

- To be shouted upon seeing an incredible mess created by a small child
- When you are groped by a TSA officer in the airport security line

*Is this how they catch the terrorists these days? **Mamma mia thatsa spicy meatball!***

MANISCHEWITZ

- All-purpose Passover curse
- The cute guy you met on JDate who turns out to be flat and bland—or sickly sweet

*I know I shouldn't date bad boys, but must I settle for a **Manischewitz?***

MANHOLE

- Someone who is walking while texting and not looking where he is going
- When you trip while walking and texting

*I almost caught a face full of sidewalk. I am officially a **manhole.***

MERCREDI *(MARE-CRU-DEE)*

- When you realize you still have three days before the weekend
- When you want to sound angry *and* French

This salade niçoise is so salty, my taste buds are vibrating. ***Mercredi!***

MOBY DICK

- When you've finally discovered just who is the biggest douchebag in the room
- When you collide with a huge white guy

Moby dick, *I think my nose is broken.*

MOFONGO

- A Latin, male hot mess
- To be moaned when kneeling before a toilet bowl

Mofongo *. . . I'll never mix rum, whiskey, and cough syrup again.*

MONTAUK MUMMERNITZ

- When you realize what you look like in a Speedo
- When you run out of gin during a hurricane

Montauk mummernitz, *we'll have to make do with Scotch.*

MOTHER FATHER

- When your child has done something that takes your breath away
- When your therapist realizes it's all been lies

Mother father! *If you knew how boring my childhood really was, you'd thank me.*

MOTHER FLOCKER

- When your local priest fails to practice what he preaches
- All-purpose duck pond swear

Mother flocker, *those mallards really think they own the place.*

See also: *Turducken*

MOTHER HUBBARD

- When your scones come out burned
- When that sweet little old lady says something incredibly filthy

__Mother Hubbard,__ she should party with Betty White.

MUMBLING MUGWORT

- When you suffer a neti pot incident
- When acupuncture just feels like needles in your back

Whoever said this doesn't hurt was clearly an armadillo.
Mumbling mugwort.

NO RASTA

- When your dreadlocks get caught in something
- When you are left out of the drum circle

__No rasta,__ dudes! That is so not mellow.

MUGGLE NUTS

- When someone trips on his broom during a college Quidditch match
- When a Prius driver revs his engine and peels out at a green light

Muggle nuts. *Maybe he has to go to the bathroom really bad.*

NOTAWESOME

- When you hear, for the eleventh time that day, someone use the word "awesome" for something that is not, by definition, awesome
- When you realize that your raw goat milk is not locally sourced

*There goes my raw-ganic-locavore status—**notawesome!***

O HENRY

- When you realize you bought that special someone the perfectly wrong gift
- All-purpose fiction-writing expletive

***O Henry,** my protagonist has gotten herself into another pickle, and expects* me *to get her out!*

OCASEK

- When your date is wearing a Member's Only jacket
- When your teenager grows six shoe sizes in a year

***Ocasek!** Perhaps I shouldn't have breast-fed him so long.*

OH, CANADA

- When you have been forced to yell at a completely polite and mild-mannered person
- When you are served a meal devoid of flavor

> *I think this is the pork . . . or did I order the turkey?* ***Oh, Canada,*** *at least it's salty.*

OH MY GARGLE

- When you are tongue-tied or stutter
- When you discover you've finished someone else's drink

> ***Oh my gargle,*** *I'm just going to assume the booze killed the germs.*

OH MY JORTS

- When another person thinks he is cool, but is not
- When you wear the improper amount of denim

> ***Oh my jorts,*** *I didn't realize this would be a formal funeral.*

OH MY GOTH

- When you bite or burn the tip of your tongue
- When entering a Hot Topic or other "mallternative" store

> ***Oh my goth,*** *that* Game of Thrones *lunchbox would be a perfect bed for my rat.*

OH MY STARS AND GARTERS

- When the cable guy doesn't show up within the agreed-upon window of time, so you leave, only to return home to find a note saying you missed his visit
- When you rip an expensive silk dress in a fitting room

> ***Oh my stars and garters,*** *I should have known a "large" in this store would really be a size 2.*

OH, PANTS

- When you get stuck in the popcorn line at the movies and miss all the previews
- When you are chased by a bull

> *I probably shouldn't have worn my bright red cape today—* ***oh, pants.***

OMELETTE DU FROMAGE *(OM-LET DOO FRO-MAZH)*

- All-purpose bistro curse
- When someone is trying hard to show off his perfect French accent

> ***Omelette du fromage!*** *If you're not careful you're gonna swallow your tongue.*

PAPPYCHINS

- To be shouted upon discovering your first gray hair
- A biker-gang leader

*Hey there, **pappychins**—I guess you think you're pretty scruffy, dontcha?*

PARDONNÉZ BLAH *(PAHR-DUH-NEH BLAH)*

- When you screw up someone's name in public
- When you are completely flummoxed by a question

*Am I secretly selling company secrets to our competitors? Uh . . . **pardonnéz blah** . . . why would you ask?*

PHILIP GLASSHOLE

- A person whose car alarm goes off repeatedly—all night
- A person who traps you into a one-sided conversation for an extended period of time, such as on a cross-country flight

*I was sitting next to a **Philip Glasshole**, so I feigned a cross between Tourette's and narcolepsy.*

PUTIN'S PJ'S / BY PUTIN'S PJ'S

- When you have drunk way too much vodka
- When a coworker annexes half your desk space

By Putin's pj's, *I draw the line at the pencil sharpener!*

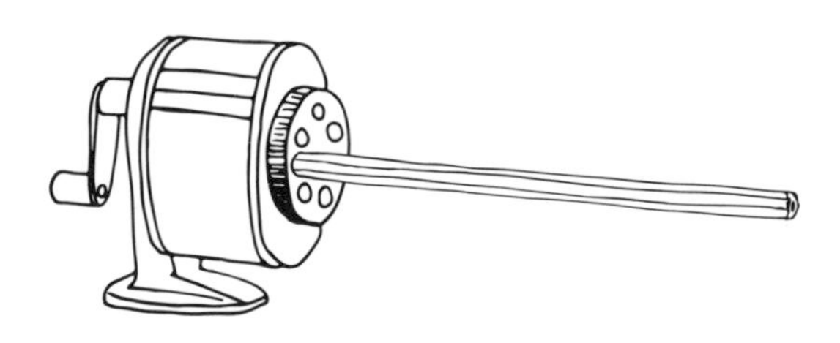

PHOOEY TO YOUEY

- When the grocery store stops stocking your favorite sweet-and-spicy mustard
- When you discover someone has left a horrible review of your business online

Whoever said the customer is always right never had to deal with trolls off their meds. ***Phooey to youey!***

PISTIL AND STAMEN

- When your flower bed is eaten by snails
- When you see the price of a dozen long-stemmed roses on Valentine's Day

Pistil and stamen! *Suddenly, the humble carnation seems a charmingly retro choice.*

PIZZLE STICKS

- When it becomes clear that the $48 special food isn't fixing your dog's internal tribulation
- When you walk into a public restroom stall and the seat is completely wet

Aw, ***pizzle sticks****—can we step it up a notch, people?*

RAMBLIN' RORSCHACH

- When an offhand comment about your mother causes your therapist's eyes to widen
- When you attempt to sketch something you're describing, and it comes out looking like a phallus

They're my favorite sea mammal, but ***ramblin' Rorschach,*** *I've never been great at drawing manatees.*

RASHIDA JONES

- When the new superhero blockbuster is sold out, and your girlfriend convinces you to see some indie rom-com
- All-purpose art house expletive

Rashida Jones, *the things I do for love.*

RICH CORINTHIAN LEATHER

- When your exposed skin hits a hot car seat in the middle of August
- When you've been suckered by a clever marketing or ad campaign

Rich Corinthian leather, *I can't believe I bought a DVD rewinder.*

RIP VAN WINKLE

- The name you call yourself after waking up from a long nap and feeling more exhausted
- To unleash an intestinal effusion that smells as if it has been festering for twenty years

*You might want to wait a minute—I kinda **Rip Van Winkled** in there.*

RIVAL DOJO

- To be exclaimed while karate-chopping a real or imaginary opponent
- All-purpose martial arts expletive

You think you're pretty fast, block-of-wood?
***Rival dojo,** take that!*

ROOFER SCREW

- When you put your foot, hand, or head through a solid object such as thin ice, a window, or roof
- When you look up and something lands directly in your eye

Is that a red-tailed hawk on top of the garage?
*Aw, **roofer screw!***

RUCKSACK

- A person a little too fond of slapping others hard on the back
- When a bear has eaten your peanut butter and toothpaste

***Rucksack**—I sure hope he appreciates fresh, cinnaminty breath.*

SADDLEBAGS

- When you pick up a box from the wrong end, allowing the contents to spill everywhere
- Unannounced guests brought to a small gathering

*Dinner would have been a lot more fun if Mary hadn't dragged those **saddlebags** along.*

SANTA AND ALL THE SAINTS

- When you mistake cayenne for cinnamon
- When you pop the button on your pants on December 27

***Santa and all the saints!** Someone could've lost an eye!*

SCHMUTZ

- Anyone who drives a Hummer outside of a war zone
- When you accidentally get sunscreen on any interior surface of your car.

*Aw, **schmutz**. This Coppertone is staining my rich Corinthian leather.*

SCHNITZEL WITH NOODLES

- When an aggressive dachshund blocks your entrance to a building
- When your bratwurst bursts on the grill

> ***Schnitzel with noodles**, I forgot to pierce it.*

SCRAPPY DOO

- When they ruin a classic TV show or movie franchise with a "cute" character
- When you step in dog poop

> ***Scrappy doo**. My Manolos are manure-los.*

Alt: *What in Jar Jar Binks*; *Shiba Inu*; *Shih Tzu*; *Shar Pei*

See also: *Cockapoo-Shih*

SHAMALAMA DING-DONG

- All-purpose celebration or party curse
- When you receive a raise from the boss you thought didn't like you

> ***Shamalama ding-dong!** Maybe he didn't see that photocopy of my boobs after all!*

See also: *Walla Walla Bing-Bang*

SHAVASANA

- When your boa constrictor and cat are both missing
- When your yoga teacher makes passive-aggressive remarks about the class's spiritual well-being

Shavasana! *Who does she think she is, Sting?*

See also: *Sweet Kundalini*

SHAZAM

- When you're on your way to the airport and see that your passport is expired
- When you change a light bulb and feel godlike at the resulting electricity

Look on my works, ye mighty, and despair. ***Shazam!***

SHEEPFLOCKER

- All-purpose farming expletive
- An absolutely horrible person

Come on, you ***sheepflocker****—buy the little girl another ice cream cone.*

SHIATSU

- When you become ticklish during a massage
- When you see the bill for your sushi dinner

Shiatsu! *Now I kinda wish the fugu* had *killed me.*

SHIITAKE MUSHROOMS

- When the oil from the stir-fry you're cooking spatters in your face
- All-purpose cooking curse

__Shiitake mushrooms!__ I'm out of EVOO!

SHIVERING SHISH KEBABS

- When you find a piece of inedible material in your food
- When you find yourself thinking carnal thoughts while in church

__Shivering shish kebabs,__ it's a good thing I've got this Bible in my lap.

SHORT PANTS

- When you realize that your new traffic shortcut has been discovered by hordes of people
- When the runner that you tripped still wins the 5K

__Short pants__—should I have worn cleats?

SHIPPING FEE

- When the boots you splurged on last week are now 50 percent off
- When you find your ATM card moments after having it cancelled

Shipping fee! *Sorry, old card—you bought a lot of junk, and never once complained.*

SHOSTAKOVICH

- When you make an error while playing piano
- When your phone buzzes during a classical music concert

__Shostakovich!__ The acoustics in this hall makes it sound like there's a vibrator in my purse.

SIR PICKLES

- The driver in front of you who stays stopped at a green light
- The person who keeps asking questions after the teacher says everyone can leave early

Come on, __Sir Pickles__, some of us have loving beers waiting for us at home.

SKUNKY JUNK

- When you must sort through the detritus in your dead uncle's basement
- When you hook up with a hippie

__Skunky junk__—your champa is charming, but it's making me sneeze.

SMOOTH JAZZ

- When you learn that a long, boring ordeal will go on even longer
- When Kenny G is playing audibly in another person's headphones

__Smooth jazz__ . . . I think I hear John Coltrane rolling over in his grave.

SNACK PACK

- A desirable person
- To engage in carnal behavior

I'd __snack pack__ with you any night of the week.

See also: *Bang Shang-a-Lang*; *Harvey Wallbanger*

SNAGGLEPUSS

- When you taste dish soap in your glass of water
- When your braces get caught on someone else's braces

I really love your One Direction poster . . . oh . . .Oh! __Snagglepuss!__

SON OF A BIEBER

- When you accidentally flip off a police officer
- When you send a sext to the wrong number

Son of a Bieber*—I think I just booty-called Uncle Irv.*

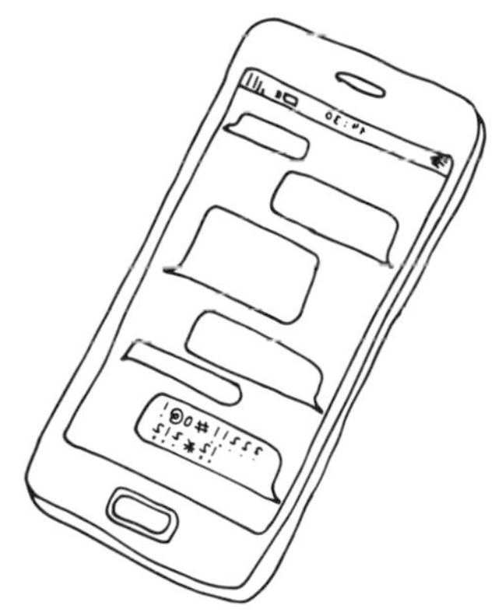

SODROLLER

- When your computer tells you it needs another eight hours and twenty-seven minutes to download your new software
- Any person who deflates your mood or throws a damper on the party

*What **sodroller** put on Counting Crows?*

SON OF A BASKET WEAVER

- When "Celebration" by Kool and the Gang gets stuck in your head for more than two weeks
- When you research a term paper and find yourself an hour later on the Wikipedia page for unusually shaped vegetables

***Son of a basket weaver**—bet my cousin Sylvia would know what to do with that gourd.*

SON OF A BEACH TOWEL

- When your partner falls asleep during sex
- When you get your first Brazilian bikini wax

***Son of a beach towel!** The ripping sound is the worst part.*

SON OF A BEGLEY

- When your no-emissions vehicle breaks down
- When your compost pile and recycle bin are ransacked by raccoons

Son of a Begley! *I* knew *Mercury was in retrograde.*

SON ON A BENCH

- When your child strikes out, hits a pop fly, or gets caught stealing second base
- All-purpose Little League curse

Son on a bench! *That second baseman's clearly a ringer from the Pony League—look at his mustache!*

SPAMHACKER

- When you accidentally waste three hours watching K-pop music videos on YouTube
- When the cat coughs up a hairball in your shoe

Spamhacker! *I see that there is a dark side to owning a Persian.*

SPACKLEHOLE

- When you hammer a nail and the wall around it crumbles
- A roommate who doesn't help to clean before you move out

*If that **spacklehole** Ernie wants his deposit back, he'd better get in that shower with a pick and mallet and start dancing.*

SPATS

- When Grandpa wanders off again
- To be uttered in the event of a jitterbug accident

__Spats!__ When I said I wanted to cut a rug, I didn't mean literally.

SPITTLE-FLIPPER

- Every bulldog ever
- When you have to carry or drive home the friend who insists she is "verrrry soberrrr"

Hey, __spittle-flipper__—if you're gonna york, let me know so I can pull over.

SPREADSHEET

- When your computer freezes, destroying the document you worked on for four hours but never saved
- Any office goody-goody and/or jerk

What a __spreadsheet.__ I just heard him offer his beach house to the boss.

SQUID LIPS

- All-purpose fishmonger's curse
- A lousy kisser

Look out for Lucinda under the mistletoe, man—total ***squid lips.***

STEPHEN KING

- When a threatening dog, car, or vampire is heading straight for you
- When you glimpse unholy doings in your next-door neighbors' backyard

Oh, ***Stephen King****—Melinda and Gary are wearing their masks again. Here comes the chanting.*

STICKY NICKELS

- When you spill soda on your computer keyboard
- When you must scrounge for change under the sofa cushion or car seat

Sticky nickels! *The writer's life is so glamorous.*

SUFFRAGETTE CITY

- When your stylist loses control of the clippers
- When you are the oldest person at the party by at least ten years

__Suffragette city,__ I have boots older than most of the people here.

SUGARFOOT

- When you drop a heavy object on your toe
- When a colleague is excessively cheerful on a Monday morning

Hey, __sugarfoot,__ can you tone it down? Some of us are still recovering from Saturday night.

SWEET BABY BUTTERCREAM

- When you catch a cupcake just before it lands frosting-side-down on the sidewalk
- When you are channel-surfing at 3 a.m. and come across *Dirty Dancing*

__Sweet baby buttercream!__ Just in time to see Patrick Swayze leap off the stage!

SWEET ANGINA

- All-purpose saturated fat swear
- When you are surprised or delighted upon being served bacon

*Chocolate cream–bacon cupcakes? **Sweet angina!***

SWEET CREAMY EGGNOG

- When your dream unexpectedly comes true, such as winning a televised contest
- When you go for a second helping and are forced to fight another for it

Ooh, ***sweet creamy eggnog,*** *gimme that!*

SWEET HOME ALABAMA

- To be uttered after downing a bourbon or whiskey shot
- Expression of general wonderment

Sweet home Alabama! *I've never seen anyone do that with ping-pong balls.*

SWEET KUNDALINI

- When you walk into a particularly foul-smelling yoga studio
- When your yoga teacher hits on you

Sweet kundalini*—that guy gives new meaning to "downward dog."*

See also: *Shavasana*

TATER TOTS

- When you are stuck behind someone using copious coupons at the grocery store
- When you're late picking your kids up from daycare

> ***Tater tots!*** *Madison and Jaden already finished circle time!*

TIDDLYWINKS

- When you legitimately lose to a small child in a game of "Memory"
- When you sneeze too hard and slightly wet yourself

> ***Tiddlywinks!*** *I wonder if can go commando in this skirt?*

See also: *Toad in the Hole*

TOAD IN THE HOLE

- When you sneeze and pass gas at the same time
- One who uses British slang incorrectly

> *You're such a* ***toad in the hole,*** *Jimmy—I don't think you even know what "fanny" means.*

See also: *Tiddlywinks*

TONY DANZA

- When you stub your toe while walking through a pizzeria
- When you discover that a friend or coworker is secretly a gifted song-and-dance man

> ***Tony Danza!*** *Now I know who's leading our* Annie *medley at the company talent show!*

TUBESOCKS

- When you get stuck in traffic due to a marathon
- When there's a two-for-one sale at the dollar store

> ***Tubesocks!*** *They've got undented cans of kidney beans!*

TUFTED TITMOUSE

- When you are attempting, unsuccessfully, to rethread the drawstring through a hoodie
- When you can't find a parking space at the arboretum

> ***Tufted titmouse!*** *Where will I charge my electric car?*

TURDUCKEN

- When you must veer to avoid waterfowl excrement on an otherwise pleasant walk
- When things get way too complicated for anyone's good

> *I guess I shouldn't have tried to attach lasers to the sharks' heads.* ***Turducken.***

See also: *Mother Flocker*

VAN DAMME

- When you injure someone in kickboxing class
- All-purpose mixed martial arts expletive

__Van Damme!__ I fear that perhaps that headbutt was ill-advised.

VOMITRON

- When your computer is overloaded with porn pop-ups from a virus
- Any electronic dance music group or fan you dislike

Why is there always one __vomitron__ who doesn't use deodorant?

VUVUZELA

- When someone wakes you up at an uncivilized hour
- A person with an annoying voice

That girl is super hot, but she's such a __vuvuzela__ I only take her to concerts.

VLAÄRG

- When you take a zinc lozenge for a cold and it messes up your taste buds for the rest of the day
- When you assemble flat-packed furniture and, despite your best efforts, the resulting item looks nothing like the catalog

I think they named this chair "Dombås" for a reason. ***Vlaärg.***

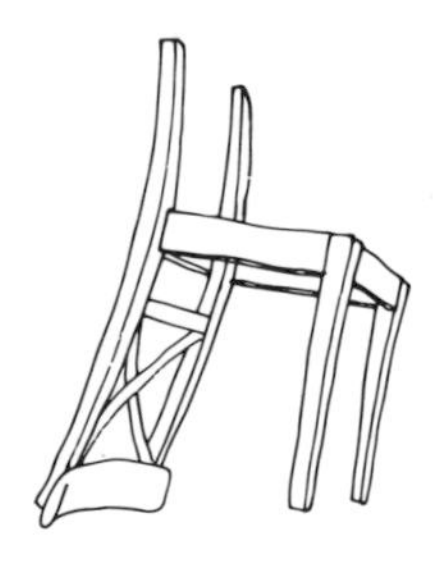

WALLA WALLA BING-BANG

- When you bowl a strike
- To be shouted in bed

> ***Walla walla bing-bang****. . . and* that's *how I roll.*

Alt: *O Epic Glory*

See also: *Shamalama Ding-Dong*

WANG DANG SWEET POUTINE

- When you have eaten too much gravy-covered fried food
- When you are kicked out of an Ottowa strip club

> ***Wang dang sweet poutine!*** *I thought it would be cool to make it rain with dollar coins!*

WASHITA RIVER

- When you experience a catastrophic GPS failure
- When the sewage line backs up

> ***Washita River****—I'm no plumber, but I don't think bathwater is supposed to be brown.*

WEE WILLIE WINKLE

- When you accidentally pee on your shoes
- A gentleman who feels the need to aggressively drive an enormous truck

Sorry about your genitals, ***Wee Willie Winkle!***

WELL, DARVA MY CONGER

- When someone from your junior high winds up becoming a reality star
- All-purpose TV-competition curse

Well, Darva my Conger*—I thought we had forged an alliance!*

WELL, DOG MY CATS

- When you keep finding poop in your yard, but you don't have a pet
- When your dog poops again, but you've already thrown away the bag

Well, dog my cats*—I wonder if I can find a big leaf lying around.*

WELL, SIP MY COCKTAIL

- When you are left with the bill
- When you are served the wrong drink at a bar

Well, sip my cocktail! *I haven't had Sex on the Beach in—oh, must be twenty-five years.*

WHAT IN PAHRUMP?

- When you break down thirty minutes outside of Vegas
- When you spot a UFO at night in the desert

> ***What in Pahrump?*** *I've never seen a shooting star zigzag before, have you?*

WHAT IN THE DICK BUTKUS?

- When you find your spouse's profile on OK Cupid
- When your uncle attempts to twerk

> ***What in the Dick Butkus****—is there a doctor in the house?*

WHAT IN SWEET BANGKOK?

- When you order panang but are presented with larb
- When capers are afoot at the local massage parlor

> ***What in sweet Bangkok?*** *I didn't realize you charged a per-limb fee for foot rubs.*

WHAT THE CHEVY VAN?

- When the pregnancy test is positive
- When you see the mechanic's estimate

> ***What the Chevy van?*** *I just got the alternator replaced last month!*

WHAT THE FIRE TRUCK? / FIRE-TRUCKIN'

- To add intensity to an expression of disbelief or dismay
- To add intensity to any expression of feeling

> *We're going to Hawaii for Christmas? That is so* ***fire-truckin'*** *awesome!*

WHAT THE L. RON HUBBARD?

- When a freaky dude in an ascot hits on you
- When you lose your car in a parking structure apparently designed by M. C. Escher

> ***What the L. Ron Hubbard?*** *It would appear my car has been lost in the fifth dimension.*

WHAT THE FAULKNER?

- When your normally eager drinking partner orders soda
- When you awaken somewhere in the South with a stupendous hangover

What the Faulkner? *I'm sure there's a great story here, if only I could remember it.*

WHOA, NELLIE

- When your sister-in-law's adorable infant claws your nose with her tiny, unclipped fingernails
- When you discover a bat, rodent, reptile, or insect in a closet or cupboard

__Whoa, Nellie!__ Is that rice moving?

WONKA DOODLE-DOO

- When you think for a second that the impossible just might be true
- When colors, patterns, and style excessively clash

She's a peach, but her taste in furnishings is a bit __wonka doodle-doo.__

WRINKLE DINKA-DOO

- An elderly creep
- When you display unfortunate shrinkage at an inopportune time

__Wrinkle dinka-doo__—I thought skinny-dipping would be cool—not ice-cold.

YAMMER TIME

- When you have put your foot in your mouth
- When the karaoke has gone on too long

*If I hear one more drunken, off-key version of "Don't Stop Believin'," it's **yammer time.***

YANK MY CRAB TRAP

- When the lobster tails you wanted to purchase for a special dinner cost $37 a pound
- All-purpose fishing boat curse

***Yank my crab trap**—I'm wicked sick of chumming.*

ZOINKS

- When the tip of a toothpick breaks off, becoming the new annoying thing lodged in your teeth
- When you blow bubbles and get soap in your eyes

***Zoinks.** I knew I shouldn't have managed this booth at the jam-band fest.*

ZAMBONI

- A dimwitted hockey player
- To slip and fall on ice

*The lake was kinda bumpy and I totally **Zamboni'd.***

INDEX

ALCOHOL & CONTROLLED SUBSTANCES

ALL-PURPOSE

ANNOYING PEOPLE

Philip Glasshole
Sodroller
What the Faulkner?

Creepy
Baby Fishmouth
Dr. Hyman
Guy Lombardo
Heavens to Betsy
Mother Hubbard
Sweet Kundalini
What in the Dick Butkus?
What the L. Ron Hubbard?
Wrinkle Dinka-Doo

Dopey
Klaphat
Manhole

Foodie
Béchamel
Cheese on Crackers
Fish Fork

Hippies, Hipsters, Poseurs
Ale-Hole / Foaming Alehole
Astral Pain
Bazooka Joe
Blah Blah Blahg
Broner
Crevasse
Funky Bunch
Homebore
Muggle Nuts
No Rasta
Ocasek
Oh My Goth
Oh My Jorts
Shavasana
Skunky Junk
Toad in the Hole
Vomitron

Irritating

Blanche, Please
Boobocrat
Chilly Willy
Chitty Chitty Bang Bang
Chucklehead
Crockpot
Dachshund
Dipstick
Jingle Brains
Juicebox
Notawesome
Philip Glasshole
Saddlebags
Sir Pickles
Sugarfoot
Vuvuzela

Jerky

Aspirin Hat
Baby Beluga
Barry US Bonds
Boobocrat
Bushtit
Crockpot
Dipstick
Fermez la Pooch
Hangnail
Junta
Putin's Pj's
Phooey to Youey
Rucksack
Schmutz
Sheepflocker
Spacklehole
Spreadsheet
Wee Willie Winkle

Snobby

Bichon
Fish Fork
François Pâté

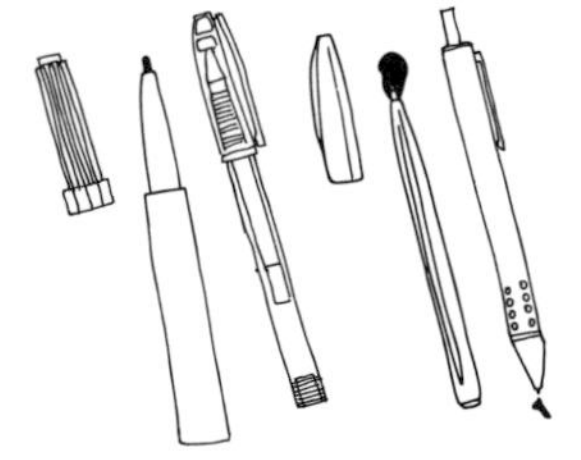

Jean Borf
Mahler Flogger
Omelette du Fromage

ARTS AND ENTERTAINMENT

Bandersnatch
Bibliohhhh
Blanche, Please
Bust My Beatbox
Chunks o' Cheese
Ducal Baubles
Fartlight
Fats McGee and his Duckies Three
Fa La La La La Lahhh
Fledermaus
Flock my Fir Tree
For the Love of Harvey Korman
Funky Bunch
Heavens to Betsy
Holy Maholy-Nagy
Kiss Maya Angelou
Mahler Flogger
O Henry
Oh, Pants
Ramblin' Rorschach
Rashida Jones
Scrappy Doo
Shostakovich
Smooth Jazz
Son of a Basket Weaver
Spamhacker
Tiddlywinks
Sweet Baby Buttercream
Well, Darva My Conger
Yammer Time

AUTHORITIES, BUREAUCRATS, THE LAW

Bacon Bits
Boobocrat
For The Love of Benji
Halliburton
Ham Hocks / Honey-Glazed Ham Hocks

Hasselhoff
Heavens to Clancy
Holy Shift Key
Junta
Shama Lama Ding-Dong
Son of a Bieber

AUTOMOTIVE (SEE ALSO: TRAVEL)

Amber Waves of Grain
Aspirin Hat
Bacon Bits
Bucking Broncos
Chitty Chitty Bang Bang
Chutes and Ladders
Dipsticks
For the Love of Benji
Geez Louise
Heavens to Clancy
Holy Mother of Madison
Holy Mothman Prophecy
In Your Hat
Klaphat
Log Jammit
Muggle Nuts
Philip Glasshole
Rich Corinthian Leather
Schmutz
Short Pants
Sir Pickles
Smooth Jazz
Son of a Begley
Sticky Nickels
Tubesocks
Tufted Titmouse
Washita River
Wee Willie Winkle
What in Pahrump?
What the Chevy Van?
What the L. Ron Hubbard?

BATHROOM

Astral Pain
Ballcocks
Blast
Chamber of Commerce
Great Beaver Dams

Great Gods of Thunder
Hot Caulking Gun
Mofongo
Pizzle Sticks
Rip Van Winkle
Tiddlywinks
Toad in the Hole
Washita River
Wee Willie Winkle

CLOTHING & SHOES (SEE ALSO: LAUNDRY)

Bust my Beatbox
Evil Tween
Gingersnaps
Haberdasher / Haberdash It
Ocasek
Oh My Jorts
Scrappy Doo
Shipping Fee

CLUMSINESS

Amber Waves of Grain
Asphalt
Ay, Kombucha
Ballcocks
Benedict Cumberbatch
Black Angus
Brad's Abs
Cannibals
Bibliohhhh
Chutes and Ladders
Cream of Broccoli
Dumfungle / Dumfungled
Fa La La La La Lahhh
Fragglerock
Halliburton
Holy Maholy-Nagy
Largemouth Bass
Manhole

Moby Dick
Muggle Nuts
Oh My Goth
Roofer Screw
Saddlebags
Schmutz
Shostakovitch
Sticky Nickels
Sugarfoot
Tony Danza
Van Damme
Yammertime
Zamboni

COWBOYS

Bucking Broncos
Flapjacks

CRAFTING

Heavens to Betsy

CRIME & ESPIONAGE

Che le Puzo
Heavens to Clancy

DAILY LIFE

Asphalt
Baby Beluga
Baby Fishmouth
Cheese on Crackers
Cul-de-Sac
Dumfungle / Dumfungled
Flubber
Fluffernutter
For the Love of Benji
Freckles
Geez Louise
Great Gods of Thunder
Haberdasher / Haberdash It

Hangnail
Hasselhoff
Holy Mother of Madison
I'll Be Jimmy-Jammed
Jiminy Christmas
Jiminy Hoffa
Jinkies
Jinx My Sphinx
Joan Crawford
Jonathan Taylor Thomas
Kiss Maya Angelou
Land o' Lakes
Log Jammit
Madame Tussaud
Mama Mia Thatsa Spicy Meatball
Mercredi
Oh My Stars and Garters
Oh, Pants
Pistil and Stamen
Rashida Jones
Rich Corinthian Leather
Schnitzel with Noodles
Shiitake Mushrooms
Shazam
Son of a Begley
Spacklehole
Spamhacker
Sweet Creamy Eggnog
Tater Tots
Vlaärg
Vuvuzela
Whoa, Nelly

DEATH

Casper the Friendly Ghost
Skunky Junk
Shavasana

DISBELIEF & AMAZEMENT

Ba Ba Rum
Bang Shang-a-Lang
Bichon
Che Le Puzo
Chimichanga
Crikey
Great Beaver Dams

I'll Be a Higgs Boson
Jinx My Sphinx
Pappychins
Pistil and Stamen
Shazam
Sweet Home Alabama
What the Fire Truck? / Fire-Truckin'
Wonka Doodle-Doo

DISGUSTING THINGS

Baby Fishmouth
Ashcan
Bazooka Joe
Cradle Cap
Dusty Bones
Fermez la Pooch
Fick
Fingerpicker
Geez Louise
Gefilte Fish
Great Gods of Thunder
Guy Lombardo
I'll be Jimmy-Jammed
Jiminy Christmas
Jumpin' Jehoshaphat
Horn of Rohan
Kibbles and Bits
Lutefisk
Madame Tussaud
Oh My Gargle
Pizzle Sticks
Rip Van Winkle
Roofer Screw
Scrappy Doo
Shivering Shish Kebabs
Spamhacker
Sweet Kundalini

Turducken
Well, Dog My Cats
Whoa, Nellie

DOGS (SEE ALSO: PETS)

Ay, Pupusa
Cockapoo-Shih
Dachshund
Doglicker
Fartlight
Fermez La Pooch
Kibbles and Bits
Pizzle Sticks
Schnitzel with Noodles
Scrappy Doo
Spittle-Flipper
Well, Dog My Cats

ELDERLY PEOPLE

Boris
By the Hornswoggle of Lord Battlesby
Crockpot
Curses
Ducal Baubles
Dusty Bones
Eat Schmaltz
For The Love of Harvey Korman
Gefilte Fish
Guy Lombardo
Heavens to Betsy
Lutefisk
Mother Hubbard
Skunky Junk
Spats
Wrinkle Dinka-Doo

EMBARRASSMENTS

Asphalt
Ballcocks
Black Angus
Blow Me Down
Bust My Beatbox
Cream of Broccoli
Dumfungle
Dusty Bones

Fingerpicker
Fledermaus
For the Love of Jheri
Freckles
Funky Winkerbean
Gadzooks
Haberdasher
Hambungle
Hot Cross Butts
Ish Kabibble
Jonathan Taylor Thomas
Jumpin' Jehoshaphat
Manhole
Kruttschnitt
Mother Father
Mugglenuts
Oh My Jorts
Pardonnéz Blah
Ramblin' Rorschach
Shiatsu
Shivering Shish Kebabs
Shostakovich
Son of a Bieber
Tiddlywinks
Toad in the Hole
Yammer Time
Wrinkle Dinka-Doo
Zamboni

FAMILY

Baby Fishmouth
Braden-Haden-Jaden
Cradle Cap
Crikey
Dusty Bones
Effuary
Ducal Baubles
Fa La La La Lahhh
Gefilte Fish
Good Gumbo
Great Gods of Thunder
Guy Lombardo
Heavens to Betsy
Lutefisk
Mother Father
Ocasek
Ramblin' Rorschach

- Skunky Junk
- Son of a Bieber
- Spats
- What in the Dick Butkus?
- Whoa, Nelly

FEAR

- Casper the Friendly Ghost
- Che le Puzo
- Cockles and Mussels
- Dorsal Fin
- Heavens to Clancy
- Hieronymus Bosch
- Holy Mothman Prophecy
- Jiminy Christmas
- Land o' Lakes
- Oh My Goth
- Stephen King
- What in Pahrump?

FISHMONGERS

- Squid Lips

FOOD & COOKING

- Ay, Kombucha
- Ay, Pupusa
- Bacon Bits
- Béchamel
- Benedict Cumberbatch
- Black Angus
- Bolshevik
- Bucket Lover
- Cheese on Crackers
- Crabcakes
- Cream of Broccoli
- Eat Schmaltz
- Fa La La La Lahhh
- Fats McGee and His Duckies Three
- Fick
- Fish Fork
- Flamin' Flaxseed
- Flapjacks
- Fluffernutter
- Gefilte Fish
- Good Gumbo
- Halliburton

Hambungle
Holy Buckets
Hot Cross Butts
I'll Be Jimmy-Jammed
Jean Borf
Jiminy Christmas
Jonathan Taylor Thomas
Jumpin' Jehoshaphat
Land o' Lakes
Little Finger
Los Zapatos
Lutefisk
Macaroni Dinner
Mother Hubbard
Notawesome
Oh, Canada
Omelette du Fromage
Phooey to Youey
Santa and All the Saints
Schnitzel with Noodles
Shiatsu
Shiitake Mushrooms
Shivering Shish Kebabs
Squid Lips
Sticky Nickels
Sweet Angina
Sweet Baby Buttercream
Sweet Creamy Eggnog
Wang Dang Sweet Poutine
What in Sweet Bangkok?
Yank My Crab Trap

FRIENDS
(SEE ALSO: SOCIAL SITUATIONS)

Boris
Broner
Chilly Willy
Good Gumbo
Spittle-Flipper

HOLIDAYS

Bob Cratchit
Effuary
Fa La La La Lahhh
Flock My Fir Tree
Frankincense and Myrrh
Gefilte Fish

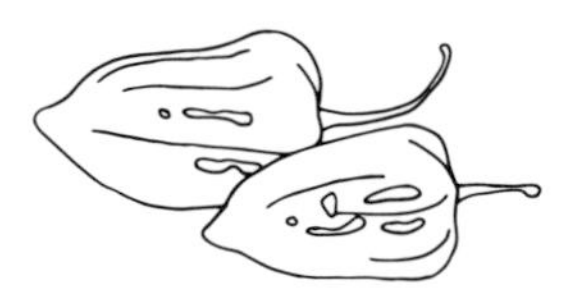

Guy Lombardo
Jinglebrains
Juicebox
Manischewitz
Pistil and Stamen
Santa and All the Saints

HORTICULTURE

Great Monocots
Pistil and Stamen

INJURIES & BODILY DISCOMFORT

General
Asphalt
Aspirin Hat
Dr. Hyman
Funky Bunch
Gimcrack
Hot Cross Butts
Rip Van Winkle
Roofer Screw
Vlaärg

Medical
Leapin' Lapendectomy
Mumbling Mugwort

Back
Brad's Abs

Eyes
Roofer Screw
Zoinks

Feet
Cockles and Mussels
Fraggle Rock
Gefilte Fish
Gingersnaps
Krakatoa East of Java
Sugarfoot
Tony Danza

Groin
Ballcocks
Blast
Cul-de-Sac

Great Beaver Dams
Kibbles and Bits
Son of a Beach Towel

Hair
Hasselhoff
No Rasta
Suffragette City

Hands
Funky Winkerbean
Jigglin' Jello

Headaches
Aspirin Hat
Blast
Chilly Willy
Hieronymus Bosch

Mouth and/or Teeth
By the Hornswoggle of Lord Battlesby
Cannibals
Gimcrack

Oh My Goth
Zoinks

Skin
Crabcakes
Flamin' Flaxseed
Rich Corinthian Leather

Stomach
Astral Pain
Chunks o' Cheese
Mofongo

INTERNATIONAL

Béchamel
Bichon
Black Angus
Che le Puzo
Deneuve
François Pâté
Kruttschnitt
Mercredi
Mofongo
Omelette du Fromage
Toad in the Hole

LAUNDRY
(SEE ALSO: CLOTHING & SHOES)

Bust My Beatbox
For the Love of Benji
Haberdasher / Haberdash It

MARTIAL ARTS

Rival Dojo
Van Damme

MIMES

Blanche, Please

MONEY

Ashcan
Macaroni Dinner
Shipping Fee
Sticky Nickels
Tubesocks
Well, Sip My Cocktail

MUSIC

Bandersnatch
Braden-Haden-Jaden
Bust My Beatbox
Chunks o' Cheese
Fartlight
Fledermaus
Funky Bunch
Good Gumbo
Shoshtakovich
Smooth Jazz
Son of a Basket Weaver
Vomitron

OFFICE & PROFESSIONAL
(SEE ALSO: SOCIAL MEDIA, EMAIL, & INTERNET)

Bob Cratchit
Boobocrat
Chamber of Commerce
Cream of Broccoli
Gadzooks
Hangnail
Holy Shift Key
Jiminy Hoffa
Jinglebrains

Junta
Kiss My Brass
Largemouth Bass
Mercredi
Putin's Pj's
Shamalama Ding-Dong
Sticky Nickels
Sugarfoot

PERSONAL APPEARANCE

Baby Fishmouth
Bang Shang-a-Lang
Blow Me Down
By the Hornswoggle of Lord Battlesby
Kruttschnitt
Madame Tussaud
Pappychins

PARENTING & CHILDREN

Baby Beluga
Baby Fishmouth
Braden-Haden-Jaden
Cradle Cap
Effuary
Evil Tween
Fraggle Rock
Gadzooks
Great Googly Moogly
Great Gods of Thunder
Holy Mother of Madison
Jigglin' Jello
Juicebox
Mamma Mia Thatsa Spicy Meatball
Mother Father
Ocasek
Son on a Bench
Tater Tots
Tiddlywinks
Whoa, Nellie

PETS (SEE ALSO: DOGS)

Chutes and Ladders
Shavasana
Spamhacker
Turducken

POLITICS & SOCIALIST REVOLUTION

Halliburton

RELIGION & PLACES OF WORSHIP

Casper the Friendly Ghost
Frankincense and Myrrh
Holy Buckets
Jupiter's Beard
Manischewitz
Mother Flocker
Shivering Shish Kebabs
Stephen King

ROLLER COASTERS

Casper the Friendly Ghost
Fats McGee and His Duckies Three

ROMANCE & SEX

Bananarama / Bananaramas
Bang Shang-a-Lang
Blow Me Down
Broner
Bucket Lover
Bucking Broncos
Chitty Chitty Bang Bang
Chucklehead
Codpiece
Dose of the Clap
Effuary
Fledermaus
Gingersnaps
Great Googly Moogly
Guy Lombardo
Grand Tetons
Ham Hocks / Honey-Glazed Ham Hocks
Harvey Wallbanger
Holy Maholy-Nagy
Holy Rick Astley
Hot Caulking Gun

- I'll Be a Higgs Boson
- Jinkies
- Junta
- Little Finger
- Log Jammit
- Manischewitz
- Ocasek
- Skunky Junk
- Snack Pack
- Snagglepuss
- Son of a Beach Towel
- Squid Lips
- Walla Walla Bing Bang
- Wang Dang Sweet Poutine
- What in the Dick Butkus?
- What in Sweet Bangkok?
- What the Chevy Van?
- Wrinkle Dinka-Doo

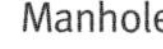

RUNES

- Horn of Rohan

SCHOOL

- Flunk It
- Sir Pickles
- Son of a Basket Weaver

SOCIAL MEDIA, EMAIL, & INTERNET (SEE ALSO: OFFICE & PROFESSIONAL)

- Bananarama
- Bushtit
- Blah Blah Blahg
- Crikey
- Effuary
- Fingerpicker
- Flubber
- Gadzooks
- Geez Louise
- Holy Rick Astley
- Holy Shift Key
- Manhole

Oh, Pants
Phooey to Youey
Sodroller
Son of a Bieber
Spreadsheet
Vomitron

SOCIAL SITUATIONS (SEE ALSO: FRIENDS)

Cheeseplatter
Crikey
Deneuve
Falklands
Flux Capacitor
For the Love of Harvey Korman
Fragglerock
Freckles
Great Googly Moogly
Harvey Wallbanger
Jigglin' Jello
Jinx My Sphinx
Joan Crawford
Mahler Flogger
Muggle Nuts
No Rasta
O Henry
Oh, Canada
Oh My Gargle
Saddlebags
Shamalama Ding-Dong
Smooth Jazz
Tony Danza
Turducken
Well, Darva My Conger

SPORTS & RECREATION

Asphalt
Ba-Ba Rum
Bah Hang Ten
Barry US Bonds
Bolshevik
Brad's Abs
Broner
Call of Cthulhu
Cannibals
Casper the Friendly Ghost

- Crevasse
- Curses
- Dorsal Fin
- Fats McGee and His Duckies Three
- Funky Winkerbean
- Gimcrack
- Short Pants
- Son on a Bench
- Walla Walla Bing Bang
- Zamboni

SUPERHEROES

- Curses

TRAVEL (SEE ALSO: AUTOMOTIVE)

- Amber Waves of Grain
- Flux Capacitor
- Geez Louise
- Grand Tetons
- Krakatoa East of Java
- Kruttschnitt
- Mamma Mia Thatsa Spicy Meatball
- Shazam
- Smooth Jazz

WEATHER

- Chilly Willy

WHITE PEOPLE

- Béchamel
- Moby Dick

YOGA

- Shavasana
- Sweet Kundalini